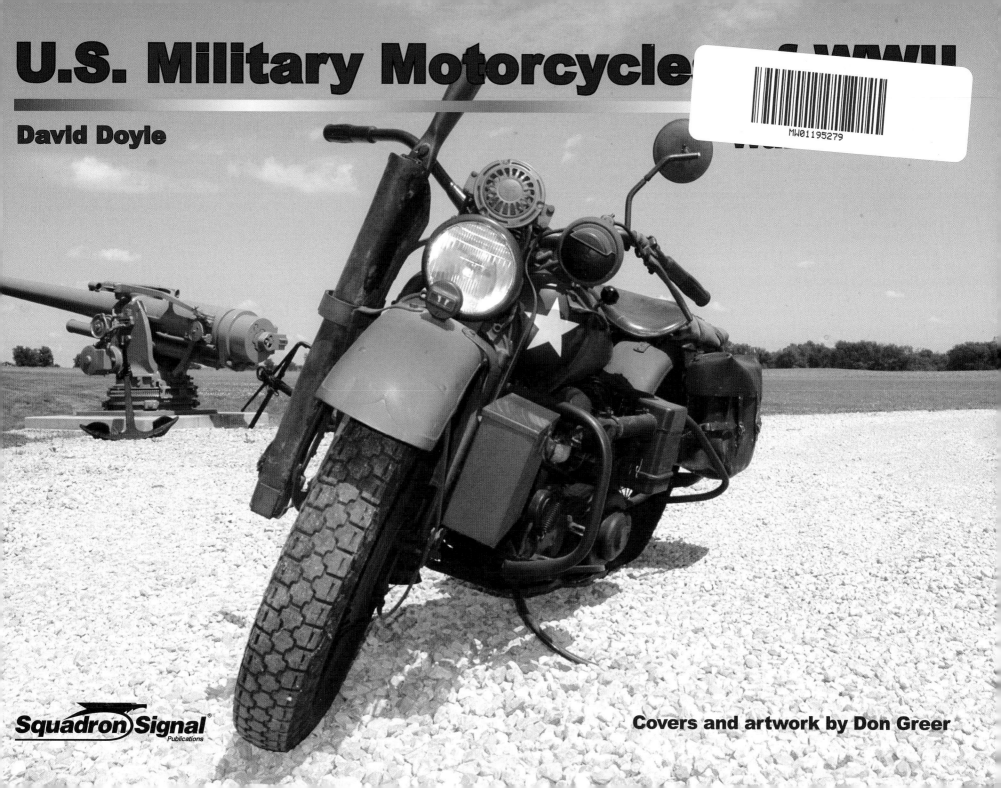

U.S. Military Motorcycles of WWII

David Doyle

Squadron Signal Publications

Covers and artwork by Don Greer

Introduction

During WWII, both Allied and Axis nations used thousands of motorcycles. Nazi Germany conscripted thousands of civilian bikes to augment its specialized military machines while the United States (U.S.) relied on the nation's manufacturing might to produce adequate stocks of motorcycles for military use by the U.S. and, to a certain extent, by its allies through the Lend-Lease program. Both Harley-Davidson and Indian produced numerous motorcycle models for the military although the advent of the Jeep significantly reduced the motorcycle's role in U.S. military strategy. In addition to its famed WLA, Harley-Davidson built the large U and UA models for sidecar work and their own shaft-drive bike, the XA. Indian produced the 340, the 741, and the shaft-drive 841.

Harley-Davidson built motorcycles for the military beginning in WWI, and the famed WWII-era WLA was simply the latest in a long series of government sales. Today, the WLA is most often what comes to mind when anyone mentions an "army motorcycle."

WLA, however, is only part of the bike's model designation. The 40-WLA and the 41-WLA through 42-WLA models are each slightly different. Army records indicate the first order for the WLA (Quartermaster Corps Contract number 7096) was placed in 1939 for 46 machines. These bikes basically were a given year's civilian WL modified with military items. The 42-WLA is what most collectors refer to when they say, "WLA." This model included military gear such as a Thompson submachine gun scabbard on the right side of the front fork, blackout lights on the front and rear, a crankcase skidplate, and a substantial luggage rack.

Prior to the U.S. Army adopting the Jeep as the standard light reconnaissance, courier, and utility vehicle, the Indian Motocycle (no "r") Company supplied large numbers of machines for these purposes. The U.S. Army ordered several Indian Chiefs or 340-Bs, powered by a 74-cubic-inch (1,200 cc) engine, and Military Sport Scouts or 640-Bs, powered by a 45-cubic-inch (750 cc) engine. Indian's 30.07-cubic-inch (500cc) V-twin 741 was popular with foreign governments, notably New Zealand, Australia, Russia, Canada, Brazil, and Britain.

Indian's model 841, a shaft-drive motorcycle was created at the behest of the U.S. Army, and was intended to duplicate the success of BMW's shaft drive motorcycles in the desert. The North African dust, grit, and sand wore heavily on conventional chain drives because their oil attracted and held the contaminants in place. In 1941, the U.S. Army ordered 1,000 shaft-drive bikes each from Indian and Harley-Davidson. Indian designed a new engine based on the Scout's 45-cubic-inch powerplant for Model 841. The angle of the block was spread from 45 degrees to 90 degrees, and the engine was mounted sideways in the frame, which gave the bike a distinctive appearance. A newly designed 4-speed foot-shift gearbox was mounted and coupled to a driveshaft. The 841's tubular, plunger-suspended frame and final drive units were much like the BMW bikes that ably served the German army in horrible conditions.

As able as the Indian and Harley-Davidson machines were, the Jeep's cargo and personnel carrying capacity destined it to overtake most roles originally filled by motorcycles. Thus the military use of bikes faded.

About the Walk Around/On Deck Series

The Walk Around/On Deck series is about the details of specific military equipment using color and black-and-white archival photographs and photographs of in-service, preserved, and restored equipment. "Walk Around" titles are devoted to aircraft and military vehicles, while "On Deck" titles are devoted to warships. They are picture books of 80 pages, focusing on operational equipment, not one-off or experimental subjects.

ISBN 978-0-89747-574-7

Military/Combat Photographs and Snapshots

If you have any photos of aircraft, armor, soldiers, or ships of any nation, particularly wartime snapshots, please share them with us and help make Squadron/Signal's books all the more interesting and complete in the future. Any photograph sent to us will be copied and returned. Electronic images are preferred. The donor will be fully credited for any photos used. Please send them to:

Squadron/Signal Publications
1115 Crowley Drive
Carrollton, TX 75006-1312 U.S.A.
www.SquadronSignalPublications.com

Acknowledgments

This book would not have been possible without the generous assistance of Brian Slark and the staff of the Barber Motorsports Museum in Leeds, Alabama; Fred and Lani Ropkey and Skip Warvel at the Ropkey Armor Museum in Crawfordsville, Indiana; Tom Kailbourn; Lee Rudd; Clark Bennett; Robin Markey, Doug Mitchell; the WWII Victory Museum in Auburn, Indiana; Francis Blake; Jerry Hatfield; Dennis Spence of Portrayal Press; and especially Denise Moss.

(Title page) The 1942 WLA was the most common military Harley-Davidson motorcycle of World War II. Several identifying features of the 1942 model are the headlight slung close to the front fender (or mud guard), the horn mounted over it, the blackout light above and to the left of the headlight, and the box-shaped air filter (below the seat).

(Front Cover) St. Lo, Normandy, France: 27 July 1944—Astride this late mid-1942 to mid-1943 42WLA, Private Roy Zimmerman of Wood River, Illinois, wears a tank helmet with MP markings, American Optical sunglasses, and leather gloves. Rather than a Thompson submachine gun, he is armed with an M1 Carbine. Pvt. Zimmerman is a member of the 507th Military Police Battalion.

(Rear Cover) Frankfurt, Germany: 1950—Sergeant Ralph W. Campbell, Co. B, 709th Military Police Battalion, poses with his Harley-Davidson WLA, the first MP motorcycle in the European Command equipped with a two-way radio. Note the skirts on the front fender, the radio box mounted on coil springs on the luggage carrier, and the chromed parts.

The Harley-Davidson WLA is the most recognized of the U.S. military's WWII-era motorcycles, but it was not the only model or brand used. Over the course of the war, WLA features changed and resulted in the 40-WLA and 41-WLA through 42-WLA models, each slightly different. This early 41-WLA has a winter windshield. Notice the high headlamp position compared to later models and the optional leg shields mounted just behind the crash bars. (Francis Blake collection)

For most, this mid-production 42-WLA comes to mind when thinking about U.S. military motorcycles. Its oil bath air filter replaced the previous and less sturdy canister type.

The introduction of the 42-WLA gave birth to the classic American military motorcycle. Beginning with registration number 611203, the headlight was relocated to this low position in the early part of the production run. Additionally, the luggage rack was constructed more substantially. (Francis Blake collection)

As the war progressed, subtle changes were made in the 42-WLA. For instance, the 42-WLA's front fender was simplified until it was essentially a curved piece of sheet metal. The engine crankcases were factory painted olive drab with black heads on the late bikes whereas previously, they were unpainted.

WWII MPs on training maneuvers pose with their motorcycles. MPs and messengers were the largest bike users in the U.S. military during the war. (National Archives)

The service headlight is mounted to a bracket bolted to the fender. Also attached to the fender are the blackout marker light, the ammunition box carrier, and the submachine gun scabbard.

The blackout headlight is mounted on a bracket clamped to the upper left side of the fork. On top of the blackout headlight is an auxiliary switch that allows the light to be turned off.

The horn and blackout light are positioned above and slightly to the rear of the service headlight. The service headlight and blackout light are both operated by the same switch that controls the ignition, and the horn button is on the left handlebar.

With its leather saddlebags and scabbard, the Harley Davidson 42-WLA was the bike most widely used by U.S. troops during WWII. This bike is what comes to most people's minds when "army motorcycle" is mentioned.

Up to the 1942 model, WLAs had molded edges on the fenders and a scalloped decoration at the front of the front fender, as seen here. Beginning with the 1944 model, plain fenders without moldings and decorations were introduced.

The left side of the front wheel shows the ammunition box carrier and fender braces. The tire's size is 4.00-18.

The blackout light is bolted to a bracket clamped to the upper left side of the fork. The gearshift lever passes through a retainer screwed to the fuel tank and includes stepped and numbered gear-shift positions. Note the two sets of recoil/cushion springs for the steering mechanism.

The brake control wire is attached to the brake lever at the upper left of the front brake. Near the bottom of the drum is the adjusting sleeve lock nut, and attached to the top of the drum with a hex nut is the brake shackle arm.

The left side of the engine shows the relative locations of the clutch pedal (lower left), carburetor (between the two cylinders) and hose, oil bath filter (right), and outer chain guard (bottom).

By applying toe pressure to the clutch pedal, the rider engages the clutch; by applying heel pressure, the rider disengages the clutch. The clutch control cable leads from the rear of the heel pad. To the clutch pedal bearing's upper right is the fuel strainer.

A three-quarter rear-left view emphasizes the placement of the front and rear safety guards, saddlebags, luggage carrier, and the twin tail light units–the service stop and tail light to the left and the blackout stop and tail light to the right.

The saddle's underside shows the seat post and saddle bar. By loosening the three bolts on the saddle bar, the seat can be adjusted to three different front-to-rear positions.

Stamped on its box is the oil bath filter's care and maintenance instructions. Note the spring clip retainers, which hold the oil cup in place, on the front and rear of the cover.

The service stop and tail light unit (left) is comprised of a service stop and tail light (top) and spare blackout tail light (bottom). The blackout stop and tail light unit (right) includes a brake-actuated stop light (top) and service blackout tail light (bottom). Both light units were mounted on a common bracket.

This view shows the top of the tail lights. The rear fender's decorative scallop identifies this WLA as an example built before 1944, when plain fenders were adopted.

In the event that the (right) blackout tail light failed, a temporary fix removed the electrical plug from the service tail light (left) and plugged it into the blackout tail light.

Saddlebags were attached to the luggage carrier by fitting studs on the backs of the bags into keyhole-shaped slots on the luggage carrier side plates. The slots are visible when the saddlebags are removed. Note the well-worn leather on the saddle of this WLA and the scabbard, which has been painted olive drab. (Doug Mitchell)

In addition to attaching to the luggage carrier's side plates, the leather saddlebags' area to the front and back had retainer straps to secure the bags on the upper frame tube and rear mudguard brace. Below the saddle bags and rear fender is the raised rear stand.

A heavy roller chain transmitted power from the gearbox to the rear wheel. Typically, this area was masked by the heavy leather saddblebag.

The saddlebags accommodate a variety of extra gear and include items such as a tool roll and a grease gun. Note the retainer strap to the front of the bag that that attaches the bag more securely to the bike.

Inboard of the kick starter pedal is the teardrop-shaped toolbox. The tall fins on the cylinder heads are characteristic of military WLAs.

The aluminum-colored, cup-shaped object in the photo's center is the ignition circuit breaker (or timer). Arrayed behind it are the four valve tappets. The engine oil feed pump is to the lower left of the ignition circuit breaker. The pedal to the lower right operates the rear brake.

The throttle grip is at the end of the handlebar's right side. The brackets securing the scabbard to the front fender and fender braces are visible.

The leather scabbard, often mounted on the WLA's front, was designed to accommodate a Thompson submachine gun with magazine inserted, but M1 carbines frequently were carried instead. The visible right tank contains 1⅛ gallons of engine oil.

The left handlebar grip controls the spark (turning grip clockwise advances spark, turning grip counterclockwise retards spark). The hand lever controls the front brake, and the horn button and the headlight dimming switch are between the brake lever and the grip.

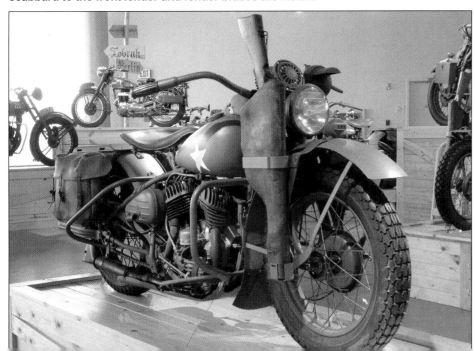

The ammunition box carrier, mounted to the front fender's left side, was designed to carry ammunition for a Thompson submachine gun. The grease zerk on the fork is to the box's right.

At the center of the steering head and handlebar is the adjustment knob for the steering damper—a friction mechanism that dampens the fork's turning action and stabilizes the front wheel at high speeds on rough terrain.

Arrayed in front of the steering head are the horn, blackout headlight, and the service headlight. Behind the lights are the upper (recoil) springs for the spring fork assembly.

The instrument panel includes a large speedometer with odometer, a green generator signal light (appears yellow in the photo and to the bottom left of the speedometer), a red oil circulation light (next to the signal light), the ignition and light switch (underneath the lights), and the speedometer light switch (underneath the ignition and light switch).

The left tank holds 3⅜ gallons of gasoline, and the right tank holds 1⅛ gallons of oil. Note the nomenclature and data plate to the front of the saddle.

The russet leather saddle is stitched. It is adjustable up and down, and it can be set to three different positions, from front to rear, to accommodate riders of different heights. Normally a rear-view mirror was attached to the left side of the handlebar.

To the front of the gasoline filler cap is the fuel supply valve. The valve is in the down position during normal operation, but when lifted, it releases a three-quart reserve supply of gasoline. Note the front hinge of the saddle, to the rear of the data plate.

This view shows the clutch control pedal and cable, air hose, left foot board, and jiffy stand below the foot board. A spring clamp secures the rubber air hose to the carburetor intake.

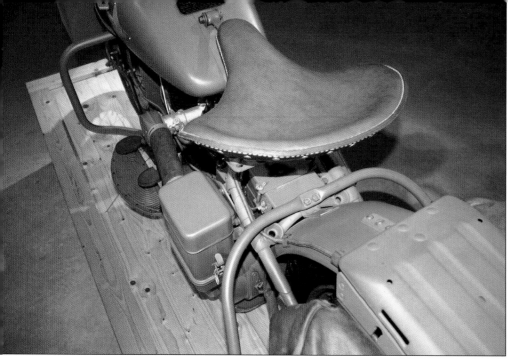

The luggage carrier details, the attachment point of the rear safety guard to the frame, the saddle, and the oil bath air filter and hose are apparent in this view. Note the battery box below the seat and the electrical cable for the tail lights that is secured to the fender.

Visible below the right edge of the saddle and on the left side of the WLA is the battery box, the teardrop-shaped tool box, the kick starter pedal and lever, and the exhaust. To the right of the photo are the oil lines, the cylinder heads, and the ignition circuit breaker.

The luggage carrier on the 1942 and later WLAs were more substantial than the earlier ones, which were frames with cross members. The operator's manual for the WLA advised checking the saddle bags frequently for cleanliness, good condition, and secure attachment to the luggage carrier.

The saddle of this WLA has been adjusted far back and exposes the saddle support bar and front hinge. Oil and gasoline lines are below the saddle.

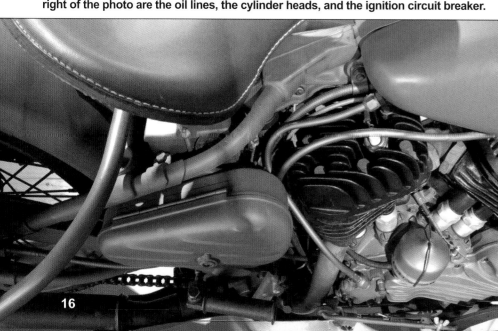

This view shows the details of the top-hinged tool box, the battery hold-down with its wing nut, and the cylinder head with military-style tall fins.

Looking down from above provides this overall view of the right side of the engine area. Visible parts on the motorcycle's right side include the right foot board, the rear brake pedal, and the front right safety guard.

The ignition circuit breaker (left) times the spark plugs' spark to coincide. Removing the aluminum-colored cap (held in place with a wire hold-down) reveals the timer head. To the circuit breaker cover's right is the spark lever, to which the spark control wire connects.

The rear brake pedal and right footboard have distinctive tread patterns. Note the rear brake rod, which is attached to the lever of the brake pedal.

The 1942 WLA weighed 540 pounds. Its total length was 7 feet, 4 inches, and its width at the handlebars was 3 feet, 5 inches. The wheelbase was 4 feet, 11½ inches. The WLA had a top speed of 65 miles per hour and a cruising range of 100 miles. The motorcycle's gas mileage was 35 miles per gallon on hard surfaces. (Doug Mitchell)

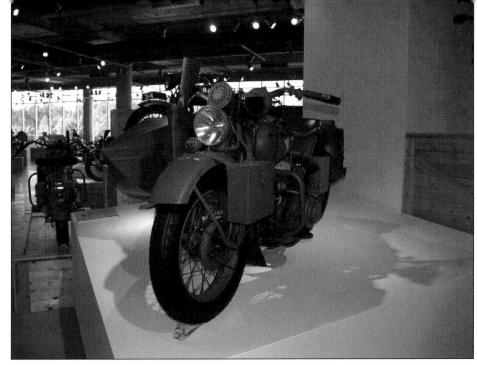

On occasion, WLAs were fitted with sidecars. Attached to this WLA is a body, manufactured by the Abresh Body Company of Milwaukee, Wisconsin, that is mounted on an LS29 sidecar chassis made by the Goulding Manufacturing Company of Saginaw, Michigan. Abresh made the bodies under contract to Goulding.

A bracket with left- and right-hand sockets is mounted on the upper rear frame of sidecar-equipped WLAs; the rear brace of the sidecar frame is inserted in a socket, which in this case is the right one. Note the battery box in front of the bracket and the rectangular oil bath filter.

This shot provides another view of the rear bracket for the sidecar. Note the black-painted engine cylinder and gray head.

The data plate on the gasoline/oil tank is the pre-1944 shape with a contoured top edge. Data plates for 1944 and later WLAs are rectangular with a straight top edge.

19

The Abresh/Goulding sidecar body has a streamlined, boat-shaped design. The front arm of the chassis attaches to the underside of the WLA's frame.

Notice the details of the sidecar body's fabrication. The front of the body rides on two small coil springs.

As viewed from the front, notice the details of the chassis frame showing the front arm. To the rear is the rear arm, and above it is the brace that attaches to the socket at the rear of the seat. Note the transverse leaf spring and bracket on the rear arm where the rear of the sidecar body rides.

Typical apparel for motorcycle troops during the war included a tank helmet. The tank helmet was not a Quartermaster-issued apparel item; it was an Ordnance-issued part of the Basic Issue Item List for the vehicle. Thus, motorcycle messengers and MPs scavenged these helmets through unofficial channels.

This view shows the lower arm of the rear chassis frame with the leaf spring attached. Above it is the chassis brace. Note the kick-starter pedal and the tool box (to the right).

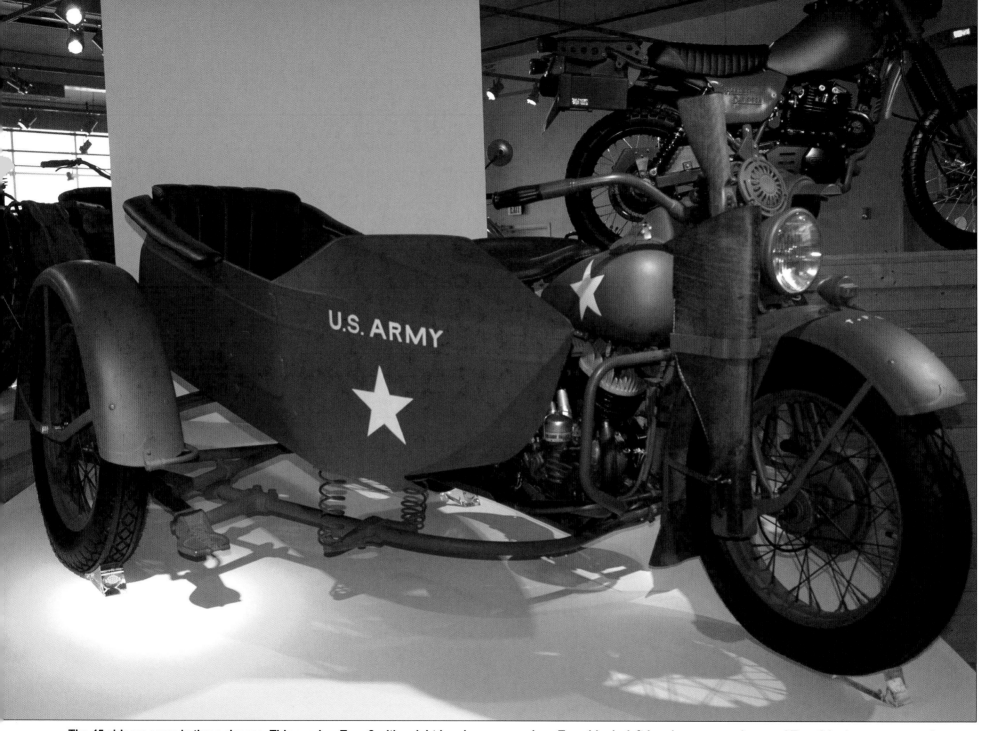

The 45 sidecar came in three classes. This one is a Type 2 with a right-hand passenger door. Type 1 had a left-hand passenger door, and Type 3 had no passenger door.

The left interior of the sidecar shows the foot rest, top of the seat back, and the leather cushion on the upper edge of the body.

Extra structural strengthening is achieved through the horizontal welt stamped into the sides of the body.

The door has two front-mounted hinges. Note the rolled edges of the body and the interior bracing.

The braces are U-shaped and are bolted to the floor. The welds joining the body panels are evident.

23

The sidecar had a leather-covered seat and side cushions. The fender was to the left.

The manufacturer's name is stamped on the step that extends from the left side of the chassis. Note the large G design with "GOULDING" superimposed over it.

This view provides details of the door, the hinges, and the side cushions. Note the rivet heads for the interior braces.

Metal-strap braces are fitted to the inner and outer sides of the fender.

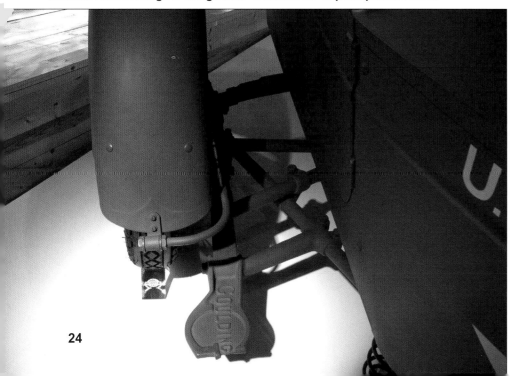

This view gives access to the underside of the sidecar chassis from the front and shows the bolt-on construction of the frame members.

The sidecar's suspension has two front coil springs and the transverse leaf spring at the rear.

As seen from the front of the sidecar, the lower bearing for the front springs, which is a split-type that bolts to the frame, is visible.

The front of the sidecar frame secures to a bolt-on bracket at the lower front of the WLA's frame.

The XA was designed with a shaft drive, in part for better operation in desert conditions. Instead of spoked wheels, the XA could be fitted with 15-inch disc wheels for desert operation. Desert-version XAs were also equipped with a supplementary shock absorber on the right fork (not visible in this photo). (Doug Mitchell)

This well-used and weathered Harley-Davidson XA was photographed in a shop at Fort Knox, Kentucky, during WWII. Note the horizontally opposed engine, the cruciform shape of the raised portions of tread, and the short height of the saddlebag compared to the Harley-Davidson U/UA and WLA.

This XA features noncharacteristic round forks and an unusual flat fender with a shortened front end. Note the placement of the horn, the headlight, and the blackout marker light atop the headlight.

Visible in this view of the left side of an XA is the fuel strainer underneath the gas tank, the cylindrical and olive drab oil-bath air cleaner; and the large battery (below the saddle). To the front of the air cleaner is the left carburetor; the XA had dual carburetors.

The tires of the XA are 4.00-18s. On the hub, the brake shackle (top), the brake camshaft lever (front), and the brake cable are visible.

The gear shifter pedal is to the rear of the left horizontal cylinder. To shift to a higher gear, the driver lifts the pedal with his toe, and to downshift, he depresses the pedal. On the right side of the transmission is a supplementary gearshift (not visible in this view). The kick starter is immediately to the front of the battery.

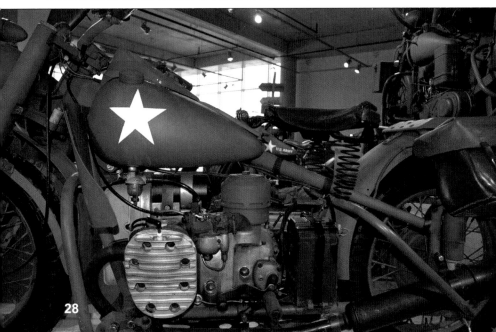

Below the gas tank (top) is the fuel strainer and fuel shutoff valve. To the rear of the left cylinder head and spark plug is the left carburetor and air manifold. The large hex nut toward the bottom right of the photo is the transmission filler plug.

Details of the left side of the transmission and the gear shifter pedal are apparent in this view. Note the metal strap hold-down for the battery, the exhaust, and the skid plate (below the exhaust).

The gas tank is a split-type with separate filler caps; each side of the tank holds a little over two U.S. gallons. The instrument panel includes a speedometer/odometer, engine indicator lights, an ignition and light switch, and a speedometer lamp switch.

The XA saddle rides on two coil springs, and the front of the saddle bar is secured to a hinge at the rear of the gas tanks. A data/caution plate secured to a recess at the rear of the gas tanks includes the manufacturer's oil, spark plug, and speed limit specifications.

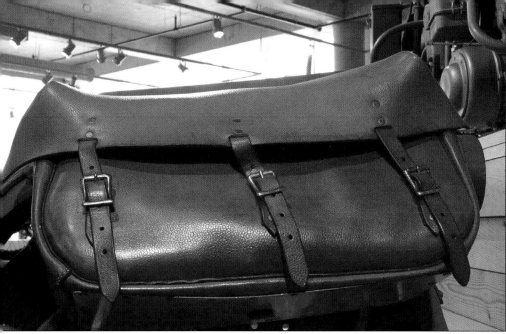

The XA saddlebags are relatively short in height. The saddlebag cover is secured with three straps and buckles. The straps are inserted into cutouts in the flap and are each attached with two rivets.

Like the Harley-Davidson WLA and the U/UA, the XA has dual tail light assemblies mounted on a common bracket. The left unit contains the service stop and tail lamp (top) and spare blackout tail lamp (bottom). The right unit includes the blackout stop lamp above the main blackout tail lamp.

The XA has dual exhausts and mufflers with "fishtail" outlets. Here, the left muffler passes between the rear safety guard and the frame, and a metal strap/bracket secures the muffler to the frame. Inboard of the muffler is the left spring suspension unit.

Noteworthy on this Harley-Davidson XA are the fairly light tone of the olive drab paint, the national stars with surrounds on the gas tank and rear fender, and the dark brown leather of the saddle and the saddlebags with lighter brown straps. This motorcycle is equipped with desert-type solid wheels.

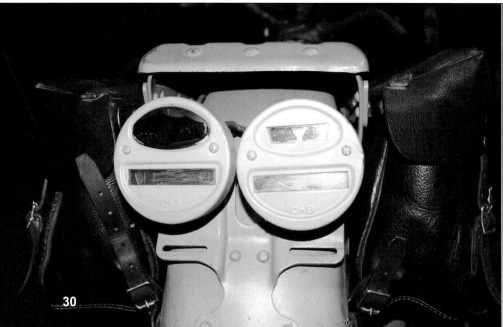

This XA is fitted out for desert operations and includes an auxiliary shock absorber on the right fork and disc-type wheels. The auxiliary hand transmission shifter is below the saddle and to the front of the drive-shaft cover. The lever on the right handlebar controls the clutch. (Doug Mitchell)

Above the muffler are the drive-shaft guard and the teardrop-shaped tool box. To the front of the drive-shaft guard is the rear brake pedal. The black cylindrical-shaped object on top of the engine is the generator.

Note the details of the rear drive unit, the spring housing, and the right muffler. This example has a simple exhaust pipe issuing from the rear of the muffler instead of the flared, "fishtail" outlet. To the rear of the rear drive unit is the filler plug for lubricant.

A metal plate is riveted to the bottom of this saddlebag. Studs on the backs of the saddlebags secured them to keyhole-shaped cutouts on the side brackets of the luggage carrier, and leather straps secured the lower front and rear of the bags to the frame.

The toolbox on the XA is the teardrop-shaped, top-hinged part that was common on WWII military Harley-Davidsons. To the rear of the toolbox is the bolt that secures the muffler bracket to the frame.

The right side of the engine area shows relative locations of the toolbox, saddle springs, auxiliary gear shifter, rear brake pedal, air cleaner, generator, and front safety guard. Below the gasoline tank's front end is the right gasoline tank shutoff and reserve supply valve. Lifting the valve straight up releases a half-gallon supply of reserve fuel.

From the right side, the transmission's attachment to the black drive hub yoke, the black auxiliary gear shifter (center), and the olive drab oil bath air cleaner (right) are visible.

The drive shaft, with the pinion shaft yoke to the rear, is visible from the right side of the XA. The lower edge of the drive-shaft guard is to the upper left of the photo. Note the support bracket for the exhaust, which is attached to the lower frame.

The heads of this XA retain their natural metal color. Sometimes, the heads were painted black. Just visible to the front of the engine is the housing for the ignition circuit breaker and the timer assemblies.

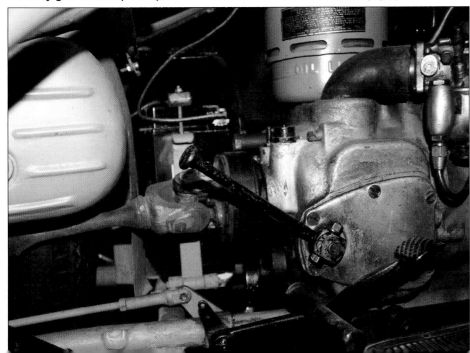

This close-up of the upper engine from the right side shows details of the air cleaner, the right carburetor (at center of photo) and air manifold, and the spark plug. A clamp-type bracket holds the generator to the top of the engine.

A simple, short front fender with atypical support brackets and round-profile forks are mounted on this XA. The front part of the skid plate is visible to the rear of the tire.

At the upper right is the right gasoline tank shutoff and reserve supply valve. Behind and below it is the housing for the timer and the ignition circuit breaker mechanisms.

This XA is fitted with a russet leather scabbard for a .45-caliber Thompson submachine gun (a rifle or carbine would also fit). A leather strap and metal buckle are provided for securing the scabbard to the mounting bracket.

In this front, three-quarter view of the same XA, the timer's ribbed face and the ignition circuit breaker cover are just visible behind the front fender.

1942
Harley Davidson
XA Military

(Above) The method of bolting the upper bracket of the scabbard to the front fender is displayed in this photo. Note the raised edging stamped on the surface of the simple, flat-section fender, which lacks rolled edges.

(Left) A head-on view of the same XA emphasizes the mounting brackets for the leather scabbard, the cruciform tread pattern of the tire, and the round cross-section forks.

(Below)The blackout marker light is on top of the service headlight. The latter is a sealed-beam unit with high and low beams. Behind the blackout marker light is the front of the horn.

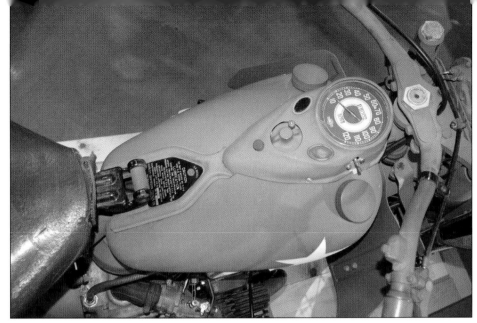

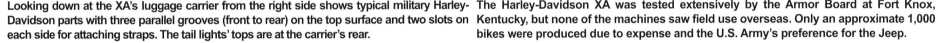

This view shows the front of the saddle, the saddle bar hinge, the data plate, the twin gas tanks, and the instrument panel of an XA. Protruding from the right handlebar and just inboard of the grip is the headlight dimmer switch.

A downward view of the left side of an XA shows (from left to right) the top of the left cylinder and cylinder head, the carburetor and manifold, the air filter, the kick starter, and the battery. The lowered jiffy stand is at the bottom of the photo.

Looking down at the XA's luggage carrier from the right side shows typical military Harley-Davidson parts with three parallel grooves (front to rear) on the top surface and two slots on each side for attaching straps. The tail lights' tops are at the carrier's rear.

The Harley-Davidson XA was tested extensively by the Armor Board at Fort Knox, Kentucky, but none of the machines saw field use overseas. Only an approximate 1,000 bikes were produced due to expense and the U.S. Army's preference for the Jeep.

This side view of the United States Marine Corps' (USMC) UA shows the cover installed over the sidecar's compartment. The cover was partially detached and rolled up when a rider occupied the sidecar. A spare tire was mounted on the rear of the sidecar. The sidecar was powered by an axle from the UA's engine. (Francis Blake)

With its 74-cubic inch, low-compression, "Big Twin" engine, the Harley-Davidson UA had plenty of power to pull a sidecar. This manufacturer's file photo of a UA, which was earmarked for the USMC, shows the sidecar, which was built by the Abresh Body Company of Milwaukee, Wisconsin. The sidecar is fitted with a detachable windshield and windshield apron. Note the tandem seating arrangement on the motorcycle. (Francis Blake)

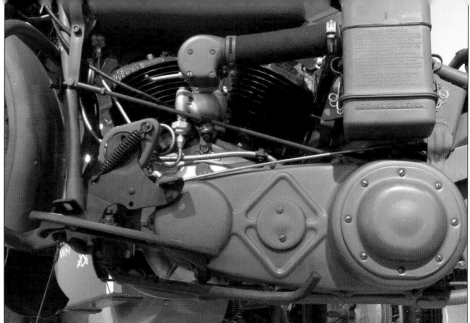

This UA, without a sidecar, features the military-type oil bath air cleaner. Mainly used for rear-area operations, the UA normally was not fitted with blackout lights or gun scabbards. This example, however, has a blackout marker light on the front fender, a scabbard for a .45-caliber Thompson submachine gun, and an ammunition box on either side of the fender for .45-caliber ammunition.

Note the front wheel, fender brackets, brake cables, and 4.50-18 four-ply tire.

Clearly visible are details of the gear-shift (on the side of the gas tank) and link rod, the clutch pedal, the jiffy stand, the carburetor, the air hose, and the box-shaped oil bath filter. Note the cautions and instructions stamped on the face of the filter.

Extending to the rear from the clutch pedal is the clutch control link. Below it is the front chain guard, which is painted olive drab. The circular cover toward the rear of the guard is the access cover for the clutch.

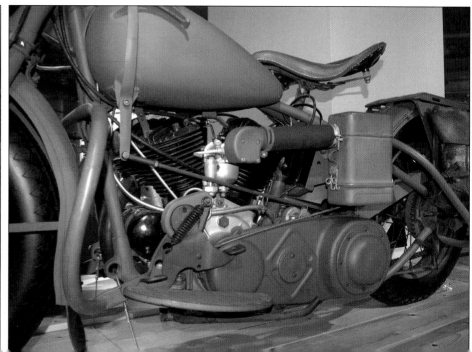

The drive chain is visible below the well-worn saddlebag. Just below and to the rear of the saddlebag is the rear stand. The battery box is immediately to the front of the rear fender.

This view provides details of the frame-to-rear-wheel, the rear safety guard attachments, the rear brake rod, the sprocket, and the rear stand.

The UA weighs 850 pounds, which is 337 pounds more than the Harley-Davidson WLA. This motorcycle stands 42 inches high and is 95 inches long. This UA example has a russet leather saddle and a luggage carrier in lieu of a tandem seat.

This UA carries an atypical submachine gun scabbard and blackout marker light on the front fender. Arrayed in front of the forks are a service headlight and horn.

The right side of the engine and the exhaust are visible in this view from the front. The bicycle-type kick-starter pedal was found on some examples. Other examples had a tubular pedal.

This view provides details of the tank (right), the saddle, frame, and the luggage carrier. The tank is a split-type with a crankcase oil compartment on the right side of the motorcycle and a gasoline compartment to the left.

To the rear of the kick-starter pedal is the teardrop-shaped tool box. It is similar in appearance to the tool boxes carried on WLAs. Note the brake pedal for the rear brake at the rear of the front safety guard.

On the left handlebar is the front brake lever. Stamped onto the cover of the horn is the Harley-Davidson shield and wings symbol. The filler cap for the oil tank is to the far left of the photo.

Francis Blake, dressed as a chief petty officer, sits in the sidecar of a Harley-Davidson U. Originally a civilian "Big Twin" Harley, the U also served in the U.S. Navy as a shore-patrol and utility vehicle. This vehicle has a blackout headlight in addition to the service headlight and bears the "SP" markings for shore patrol and a navy registration number stenciled on the gas tank. (Francis Blake)

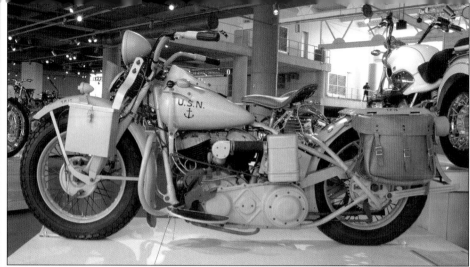

This museum example of a Harley-Davidson U lacks the sidecar. It carries a scabbard for a Thompson .45-caliber submachine gun and an ammunition box carrier for .45-caliber clips on either side of the front fender. A blackout marker light is on top of the fender.

This view emphasizes the U's 4.60-18 tires, gas tank–mounted gear shifter, and details of the front brake. Under the service headlight is the horn, and the small mud flap is at the bottom of the fender. The round socket, on the front of the frame and just above the footboard, held the sidecar's front brace when it was installed. Each side of the frame had a socket.

As seen from the left side, the layout of the U is very similar to that of the army's version, the UA. The frame and sheet metal parts are painted light gray. The engine cylinders are black, and the heads retain their natural metal color.

The ammunition box carrier has two hinges on the inboard side and a simple latch. The tire pressure specification, "T.P. 14," is lettered on the side of the fender. Mounted to the gas tank is a sheet metal guide with stepped cutouts for shifting positions. The gear shift lever passes through the sheet metal guide.

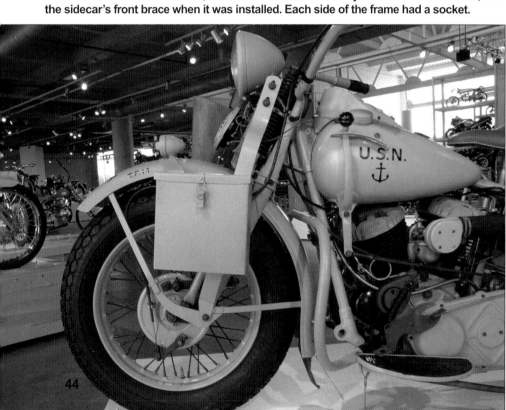

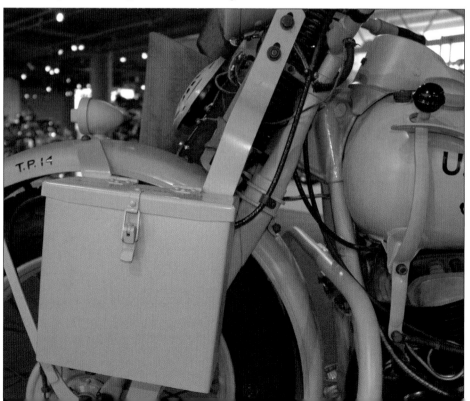

The brake shackles at the top of the brake drum have red grease-gun fittings at each end. The brake cam shaft also has a grease fitting. The brake lever attaches to the brake cam shaft toward the bottom of the brake.

The saddlebags had studs placed on their backs to secure the bags to the sides of the luggage carriers. Leather straps on the sides of the saddlebags held them down. Note the box-shaped oil bath air filter to left, and the "T.P. 16" tire pressure specification on the rear fender.

The gear shift link extends from the bottom of the shift lever. The transmission is a three-speed. The clutch pedal is above the foot board. Extending to the rear of the clutch pedal and along the top of the forward chain cover is the clutch control cable.

At the center of the rear wheel is the brake sleeve nut. To the left of it in the photo (or, toward the front of the vehicle) is the left adjusting screw. An adjusting screw is on each side of the wheel, and they are used for controlling the chain tension and aligning the wheel. At the bottom of the wheel is the brake operating lever and control link.

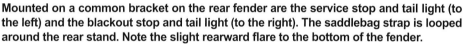

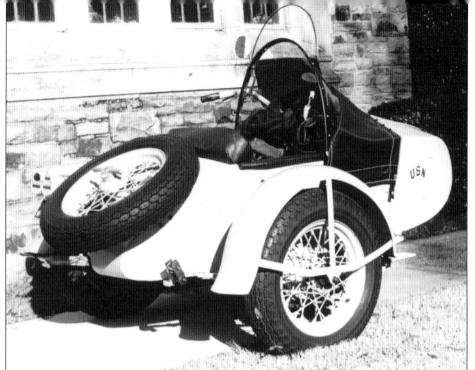

Mounted on a common bracket on the rear fender are the service stop and tail light (to the left) and the blackout stop and tail light (to the right). The saddlebag strap is looped around the rear stand. Note the slight rearward flare to the bottom of the fender.

The service stop and tail light unit (left) includes a service stop and tail light at the top and a spare blackout tail light below it. To the right of the unit, the blackout stop and tail light has a brake-actuated stop light at top and service blackout tail light at bottom. This museum example of a Harley-Davidson U bears the markings of Agana Naval Air Station, Guam.

This U.S. Navy Harley-Davidson U sidecar has a windshield and dark canvas windshield apron attached. To the rear of the windshield, the cover for the passenger's compartment is rolled up. Note the fender braces, which are fabricated from thin steel, and the leaf-spring shackle behind the fender.

This shot gives an overall view of the right side of a model U. The motorcycle has a 59.5-inch wheel base, almost 9 inches longer than the wheel base of the Harley-Davidson WLA. The bigger and heavier U had a top speed of 55 miles per hour, which was 15 miles per hour less than the maximum speed of the WLA.

This museum example model U features U.S. Navy shore patrol markings and a light gray paint scheme. Typically, the model U sidecar's rear deck held a spare tire. (Denise Moss)

Nestled in the frame, below the saddle, is the oil tank. Unlike the WLA, which incorporated the oil tank next to the gasoline tank, the U (and UA) model has a separate tank. Viewed from above, it is U-shaped with a center cutout to accommodate the battery.

The teardrop-shaped tool box, mounted on the rear right side of the frame, has a piano hinge at the top. The strap secures the front of the saddlebag to the rear safety guard.

The exhaust features a distinctive, flared opening at the rear. Note the drive chain and the right wheel adjusting screw at the hub.

The right side of the U model shows the oil tank, the kick-starter crank and pedal, and the exhaust. The spring at the base of the starter crank returns the crank to upright after it has been kicked downward to start the engine.

The heart of the U (and UA) was the 74 cubic-inch displacement flathead twin. The side-valve V could push the motorcycle and sidecar to 55 mph. This engine was used to power most large Harley-Davidson bikes, civilian and military, from 1937 through 1948.

Looking down at the engine's right side, the oil pump is to the lower left, and the ignition circuit breaker is to the left of center. The spark control wire is in between the cylinders, and the end is attached to the spark lever to the right of the ignition circuit breaker cover.

The inverted-cup-shaped object between and outboard of the cylinders is the ignition circuit breaker (or timer). Behind it are four valve tappets. Above the right foot board is the rear-brake pedal.

The Thompson submachine gun scabbard is affixed to brackets, which are attached to the left side of the fork and the fender brace. A small strap with buckle at the bottom of the scabbard secures it to the lower bracket.

A tire pressure caution is stenciled on the front fender's right side. Note the Agana NAS marking on the front fender and the registration number painted on the rear fender's front.

This Harley-Davidson U was fitted with a rear license plate. Between the sidecar and the motorcycle is the sidecar's left leaf spring. Instead of the box-shaped oil bath filter, this example has a cylindrical air filter, visible below and to the left of the saddle.

The foot rest in this sidecar is a horizontal tube mounted on brackets. An M1 carbine is stored in a scabbard on the left side of the interior. The passenger's compartment cover is roughly rolled up and stored below and to the rear of the windshield.

The windshield of the sidecar of a U-model Harley-Davidson has been tilted forward to give the passenger more room to enter the sidecar. The butt of a rifle or carbine is protruding from the left side of the passenger's compartment. The studs on the side of the car are for fastening the windshield apron and the passenger's compartment cover which, in this case, is rolled up below the windshield.

This close-up shows the details of the U-model's headlight.

The sealed-beam headlight and the front of the horn are visible. The gear shifter knob is visible to the left.

The submachine gun scabbard, blackout marker light, headlight, siren, and .45-caliber ammunition carrier box are all visible. The front of the mounting brackets for the scabbard and ammunition carrier are attached to the fender with large screws. The rear of the brackets are attached to the forks on either side of the headlight.

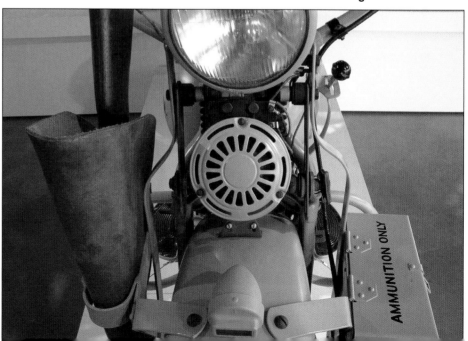

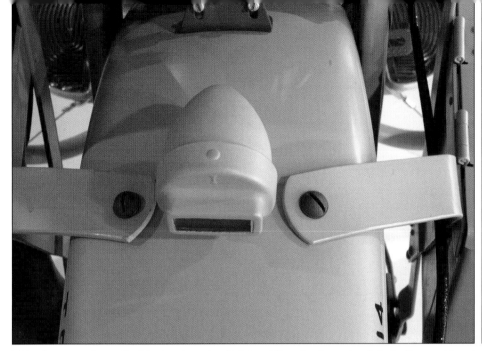

This close-up shows the blackout marker light and the attachment points for the scabbard and ammunition carrier brackets. At the top of center is the base of the bracket for the horn, which mounts to the fender.

The butt stock of a .45-caliber Thompson submachine gun protrudes from the scabbard of a Harley-Davidson U. Though designed to hold a Thompson with an ammunition clip inserted, the scabbard also could accommodate rifles and carbines.

Wiring for the horn, headlight. and front brake cable are visible in this view. Note the thin profile of the gearshift lever to the right. Also note how the rear bracket for the ammunition carrier is attached with two bolts to the upper fork.

A downward view from the left side of the Harley-Davidson U-model shows the gear shift guide mounted to the gasoline tank. Also visible are the foot board, the clutch pedal, the oil bath filter, the air hose, and the carburetor air inlet.

To the front of the left gas cap is the fuel supply valve. Normally, the fuel supply valve is left in the down position during operation, but when it is lifted, the valve releases a three-quart reserve supply of gasoline. A data plate is affixed to the rear of the gasoline tank.

This saddle is tanned leather with white stitching around the edge seam. Below and outboard of the edge of the seat are the two clamps that secure the bracket for the air filter to the frame.

To the front center of the instrument panel is a large speedometer with odometer. To the rear left of it is the green generator signal light, and to the right is the red oil circulation signal light. To the rear of these lights is the ignition and light switch, and to the rear of it is the speedometer light switch. Above the right gasoline cap is the odometer reset.

The seat's underside shows its attachment to the saddle bar with bolts. The seat post allows up and down adjustment, and the seat also adjusts forward and to the rear.

As viewed to the front from over the luggage carrier, the battery box is nestled into the recess in the center of the oil tank, located below the saddle. To the left on the oil bath air filter is the rear retaining clip. Releasing the rear and front clips allows the oil cup to be released for disposal of the old oil and replenishment with fresh oil.

This view shows details of the kick starter, the tube-type starter pedal, the kick starter spring, the exhaust, and the muffler. To the top left is the right side of the oil tank, and to the lower left is the bell crank for the crossover of the rear brake operating rod.

This close-up view providess details of the the battery box and its cap, which is secured in place with wing nuts. Note how the oil lines enter the front of the oil tank, which encloses the battery. Also note the louvers on the inner face of the oil bath air filter body.

This downward view shows the right foot board with its distinctive, concentric non-skid pattern on the rubber pad. Note the round socket on the front of the frame. This socket accommodates the front attachment brace of a sidecar.

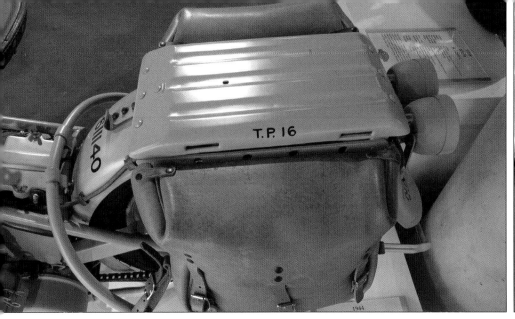

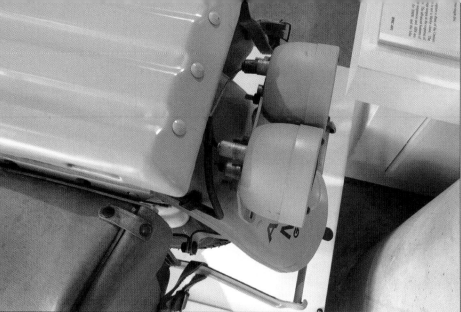

The battery cover, rear safety guard, luggage carrier, saddlebags, and twin tail light assemblies are all visible in this left-side view of a Harley-Davidson U.

Note the three wide grooves on the luggage carrier's upper surface, the electrical cable for the tail lights, and the wiring sockets on the rear of the tail lights.

The U.S. Navy's Shore Patrol was the biggest military customer for the Harley-Davidson model U.

The Indian 340-B was the civilian Indian Chief motorcycle as adopted by the U.S. armed forces. This hefty motorcycle weighed 550 pounds, had a 62-inch wheelbase, and was similar in size to the Harley-Davidson models U and UA. The 340 had an Indian V-2, 72-cubic-inch engine capable of producing 40 horsepower. The 340-B generally was configured with a sidecar. In some instances, however, the bikes were used for Military Police duties without the sidecar for improved performance.

A distinctive leaf spring was incorporated into the front suspension of the 340-B. A blackout light is mounted on the front fender, and the headlight and a siren are on the fork. The saddle is mounted on a post with an internal spring that has adjustments for tension as well as adjustments forward and aft. The cylinder below the seat is the oil bath air cleaner. The vertical cylinder at the rear axle is the slipper cylinder, which houses the rear suspension's left spring.

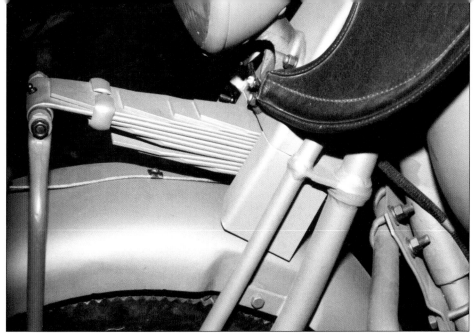

This shot gives a detailed view of the front leaf spring. Note the zerk for lubricating the spring-end bearing. The electrical line for the blackout headlight is on top of the fender. The fender is indented at the point where the fork passes and bolts to it.

In this photo of the engine's left side is the clutch shift pedal and clutch, the rubber covered foot board, the carburetor, the air hose, and the oil bath air cleaner with a caution plate identifying it as a Houde product. The black box below the air cleaner is the battery.

The fuel tank had a 3½-gallon capacity. Below the tank are the cylinder heads, which are unpainted cast aluminum. The cylinders and the carburetor are also below the tank. The rubber air hose is secured to the air intake with a clamp. Note the metal clamps that retain electrical wires to the frame at the lower left.

Recommendations were made to clean the air filter and to change the oil in the oil bath every time the engine oil was changed, and these tasks were recommended to occur more often when operating in particularly dusty conditions. Note the unpainted cast aluminum clutch housing and the manner in which it is bolted to the mounting flange on the frame.

To the lower left of the rear wheel and suspension (viewed from the left side) is the battery. Note the slipper cylinder's details and its bolted mounting to the frame. The center axle nut passes through the flange at the rear of the cylinder's center. Loosening this nut allows the rear wheel to be moved forward or to the rear for drive chain adjustment.

A combination tail light/brake light is bolted into place on the rear fender of the Indian 340-B. A blackout tail light is placed above this combination light unit. Small brackets are screwed onto the fender in order to retain the electrical lines for the lights.

A powerful machine, the Indian 340-B was ideally suited for side car work, however the sales volume for this motorcycle remained low.

The right side of an Indian 340-B shows the exhaust system as well as the chain guard. Shifting gears was achieved with a shifting lever next to the fuel and oil tank. The shifting link to the transmission is visible, and a billy club is affixed to brackets on the front fork to keep the military police "character" of this vehicle.

This view is of the Indian 340-B from the front right. The shift lever feeds into a bearing located beneath the fuel/oil tank. Just to the front of that bearing, note how the front leg guard is secured by U-bolts to a mounting plate on the front of the frame.

Visible in this shot are further details of the right rear of the 340-B. In particular, the drive chain, the chain guard, the slipper cylinder, and a small tool box with a lock are highlighted. Note the riveting (barely visible) of the russet leather saddle cover to the saddle.

To the upper right is the black shifting lever and the shifting link rod that connects the lever and transmission. The fuel tank's right side housed an oil reservoir in front and a reserve fuel tank at the rear. The oil tank was a dry-sump lubrication type that pumped sufficient oil to the engine for lubrication and served as a repository for the returned excess. The distributor is on top of the oil pump, and the rear brake pedal is at the lower right.

This view shows the Auto-Lite distributor, exhaust manifolds, and transmission shift link rod.

The Indian 340-B had internal-expanding type brakes. The front brake was controlled by a hand lever on the right end of the handlebar. Shown here is the front brake from the right side with the brake cable attached to the brake arm at the bottom of the brake drum plate. The tires were 4.50-18s.

This view shows the distinctive leaf spring of the front suspension. Note the spring clip as well as the zerk at the spring end bearing. Greasing the bearing was recommended every 200 miles. The horn is stamped "INDIAN" above the center louvers. The headlight bracket is unpainted metal, and the up and down tilt of the headlight was adjustable.

The switch on the left handlebar is the high-beam/low-beam switch for the headlight. The left handlebar grip is the throttle control, and the right grip is the spark control. The ammeter is the small gauge to the right of the cap for the main gas tank. Below the ammeter is the speedometer. The olive drab control to the right of the ammeter is the ignition and light switch, to the right of which are the oil (front) and reserve gas tank (rear) caps. The nomenclature plate identifies this bike as a model 74-340, cautions that, "No additional equipment will be added on this motorcycle," and gives specifications for top speed, oil types, and spark plugs.

This unmarked 340-B with attached side car was tested at the Holabird Quartermaster Depot in 1941. However, by this time the Bantam Reconnaissance Car had been extensively tested in many of the same roles, and this vehicle was found to be generally superior. Thus, procurement of the 340-B was limited, and the primary users of this motorcycle were Military Police and messengers. Three years later, in 1944, a further group of essentially identical model 344-B bikes (the last two digits of the model number represent the design year) were procured. This procurement was the last large order that Indian received from the U.S. military.

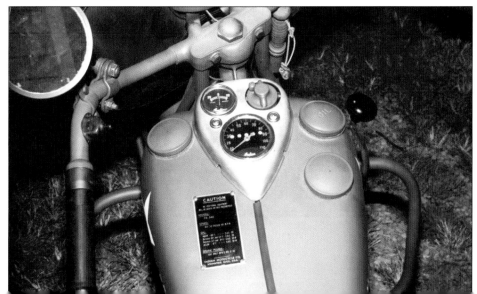

An upper view of an Indian 340-B, assembled mostly from NOS parts, emphasizes the rugged construction of this warrior. This example lacks the front and rear leg guards seen on the previous 340-B. (Robin Markey)

The Indian Model 841 was a shaft-driven motorcycle that was similar in concept to the German BMW R71. Although this bike was developed for desert warfare, the 841 never saw action in WWII. Instead, a few of approximately 1,000 examples manufactured were used for testing or training, and the rest were sold as unused surplus. The Model 841 weighed 550 pounds and had a wheel base of 59½ inches. (Jerry Hatfield)

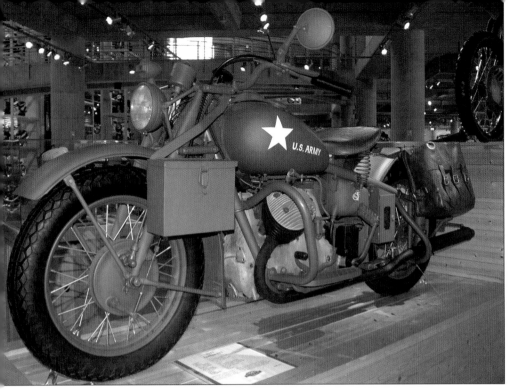

The 841 was considerably different in layout than the Indian 340-B. The most prominent variation in this view is the 45-cubic-inch Indian Scout V-2 engine with its cylinders set at 90 degrees rather than 45 degrees on the civilian version of the engine. The bike had dual exhausts and mufflers, one on each side, as opposed to the single exhaust and muffler on the right side for the 340-B. Also, the oil bath air cleaner was less prominent and was seated slightly farther forward.

Projecting from the brake plate above the attachment points for the fender braces are the speedometer drive and cable. Just below the speedometer drive is the axle nut.

The 841's brakes were the internal-expanding type. The front brake also was a non-dragging type that, when properly adjusted, was designed not to lock the wheel. This brake was operated by a hand lever on the left handlebar. Notice the brake cable and its attachment to the brake arm.

The blackout marker light is attached to the top of the headlight with a piggyback mount. The speedometer is to the rear of the blackout light. The front fork springs are visible; the vertical coil springs were a departure from the Indian 340-B's leaf-spring front suspension.

This view gives a close-up of the 5-inch sealed beam headlight, the blackout light, speedometer, and the front fork springs. Note the brake and speedometer cables.

The Indian's cylinder head, carburetor, air intake elbow, and oil bath air cleaner are all visible. Below the oil bath air cleaner is the engine case. The kick starter is to the case's rear, and the oil tank, with its oil lines connected to the tank's bottom, is above the kick starter. The battery is below the oil tank. Note the front safety guard, the foot board, and the tool box. Shifting was achieved through a foot lever with front and rear foot pedals, visible above the footboard.

This view provides a detailed look at the front fork, part of the front of the frame, and the left cylinder head with spark plug and wire. The black cylinder below the front of the left gas tank is the ignition coil.

This close-up of the left side of the engine shows the braided ignition wire and the left carburetor (with markings of the L & L Manufacturing Company from Indianapolis, Indiana). Below the carburetor are the gasoline line and the olive-drab gas filter. The filter bowl could be removed for periodic cleaning. Note the foot shift pedal at the bottom of the engine case.

Left to right are the fuel line, air cleaner, kick starter pedal, oil tank, battery (below the tank), and tool box. A caution plate on the tool box door provides data on lubrication, maximum speed (65 mph), spark plugs ("Use only Indian TM 44264"), and location of operating controls. Note the mounting bolt, at the rear of the gas tank, that attaches the tank to the frame.

This view shows the brake plate, front fender and brackets, safety guard, and exhaust. The brakes could be adjusted by turning a nut at the brake arm connection (bottom of photo) or at the cable-stop screw at the brake plate's upper side. For further adjustments, the brake arm could be removed from its serrated shaft and repositioned at a different angle.

The kick starter lever, pedal, and housing are highlighted in this view. The driver would turn on an ignition key at the center of the instrument panel on the tank and then kick down on the pedal until the engine started. The coil spring at the pivot end of the kick starter lever returned the lever to the upright position when the driver released foot pressure from the pedal. To the left of the kick starter is the rear pedal of the shift lever.

Leather saddle bags were mounted on each side of the rear fender. Note how the exhaust is routed through the rear safety guard. Just visible below the saddle bag is the left spring frame slipper, which housed the left rear suspension spring.

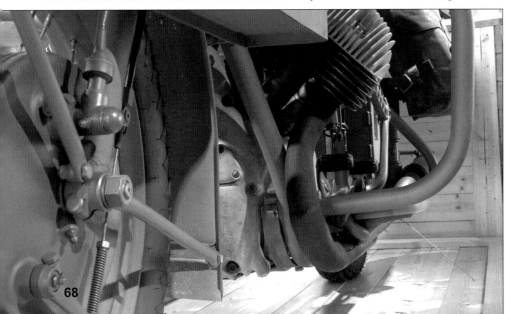

Although the military did not widely use the 841, many people, including a former president of Indian, believed this bike was one of the best products Indian made.

This shot provides a close-up of the 841's left saddlebag.

The blackout tail/brake light (top) and tail/brake light (bottom) are mounted on a common bracket on the rear fender. The electrical cable for the tail lights is fastened by bolt-on clips to the left side of the rear fender. The operator's manual stressed exercising great care when attaching the light cables to their proper brackets so that crimping or breaking the cables while operating the motorcycle could be avoided.

The vertical cylinder located to the rear of the muffler is the left spring frame slipper. The axle passes through the flange to the right (or rear) of the cylinder's center. The holes through the hub provided access to the wheel stud nuts with a long hex wrench.

The blackout light is standard U.S. government issue, and it comprises a sealed unit with the bulb, the filter element, and the blackout mask inside. By removing the screws, the cover (or "door") can be taken off, and the light and other elements can be replaced.

This overall view of the Indian 841's left side reveals the power train, from the transmission below, the rear of the cylinder, the drive shaft, and the rear drive housing. Below the seat springs is the oil tank with its prominent filler neck and cap. The tank capacity was three U.S. quarts. The gas tanks, one on each side, each held 2½ U.S. gallons. (Jerry Hatfield)

The front of the final drive housing shows the drive shaft connection. The 841-model featured a pinion and ring-gear drive. A drive shaft was incorporated into the design instead of a drive chain because the vehicle was intended for desert service, where a drive shaft would hold up better under sandy conditions than a chain.

This shot emphasizes details of the right saddle bag, the final drive, and the right muffler. The mufflers and exhaust pipes are separate parts, and either unit can be removed without disassembling the entire exhaust line.

The rear mount for the right muffler is evident in this view. Note the hex bolt that attaches the muffler to the frame. Above the muffler is the rear drive housing. The drive (or propeller) shaft runs from the rear drive housing to the four-speed transmission. The right spring frame slipper, like its counterpart on the left side, includes a flange to accommodate the rear axle. Note the axle nut.

This view shows the tail/brake lights from the right side. Note the threaded mounting studs and nuts and the electrical connections.

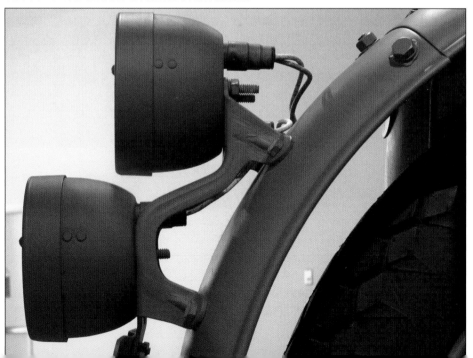

The battery is the black box at the center. To the front of the battery are the drive shaft and the dust cover seal that protects the universal joint at the rear of the transmission.

To the oil tank's right is the Houde oil bath air cleaner with a data plate instructing how to service the cleaner. The right air intake elbow and right carburetor are to the air cleaner's right. The rear brake pedal is above the footboard. Barely visible above the carburetor is part of the Auto-Lite GDE-4810 6-volt generator with data plate and the Auto-Lite distributor. Note that the gas tank's bottom is sculpted to clear the distributor.

The right leg of the center stand, with its spring return, is just inboard of the lower frame. The center stand was used to prop the motorcycle up in a vertical position. For general parking of the Model 841, a kickstand was placed under the right footboard.

This right-side view provides a close-up of the oil bath air cleaner, its data plate, and the carburetor. Projecting out and downward from the side of the carburetor is the choke lever, which was linked with the choke mechanism on the left carburetor so that lifting the lever actuated the choke on both carburetors.

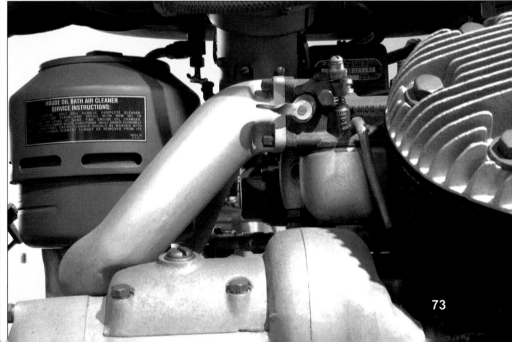

Details of the front suspension are emphasized here. Two side links on each side of the front forks are called fork shackles, and they tie the forks to crossbars on the steering mechanism on the top and bottom of the fork head. Shock absorption in the front end is provided by two springs on either side of a single shock absorber. The large black knob projecting up from the steering head is the steering damper, which tightens the steering action when fast, hard riding is necessary.

The saddle cover is russet leather and was riveted to the saddle. The front of the saddle is pivoted to the fuel tank and rides on two coil springs mounted to brackets on either side of the frame.

The Model 841's front wheel is the roller-bearing type. Access to the lug nuts for the wheel are through the holes around the hub. The motorcycle's horn is in the angle below the apex of the front of the frame and to the rear of the fender.

The raised panel on top of the fuel tank holds a generator charge indicator (left), oil pressure indicator (right), and ignition-light switch (lower). The right and left gas tank each have a cap. The right grip on the handlebar is simply a grip, not a spark controller, since the Model 841 had automatic spark control. The right lever is the hand clutch control. The left handlebar grip is the throttle control, and the left-hand lever controls the front brake. A headlight high-beam switch is also on that side of the handlebar.

The Model 841's front forks are fabricated from tapered tubing with an oval cross section. The frame tubing is fabricated from round cross section. The tire sizes are 4.00-18s, and the bikes received either the Firestone or Goodyear brand tire at the factory. The 1942 maintenance manual noted, however, that any tire with the same dimensions that met government specifications could be substituted. (Jerry Hatfield)

The left gasoline tank with the cap and lights/switch panel is viewed from the side. Note the clamping-type right mounting bracket for the handlebar.

This view looks over the twin gas tanks. The panel for the indicator lights and ignition/lights switch is at the center, and the filler caps are on either side. The damper knob projects from the handlebar's center. The handlebar is clamped to rubber shock mounts to buffer the amount of road shock transmitted to the driver's hands and arms.

The diamond tread pattern on the 4.00-18 front tire and details of the front of the brake drum are evident in this photo. Protruding from either side of the frame are the front safety guards.

This front view shows the service headlight and blackout front marker light. The service headlight was a 5-inch sealed-beam model. Both lights had removable covers to allow replacement of the bulbs. The speedometer is to the right of the blackout marker.

This downward look shows the left foot board, the left cylinder head at left, the fuel filter to the right of it, and the transmission gear shift pedal below. To shift to higher gears, the driver tapped the heel pad (to the right), and to downshift, he tapped the toe pad (right).

Note the stitching on the edge of the leather saddle cover, the details of the saddle itself, and the manner of its mounting on a bracket. The rear of the gas tanks are indented to accommodate the front of the saddle. Just visible to the lower right is the front of the luggage carrier rack.

The kick starter, the oil tank, the battery, and the tool box are visible from the right side of the motorcycle. The kick starter's pedal swings out of the way when it is not in use. The large screw on the kick starter housing, which is to the left of the coupling under the oil tank, is the filler plug for lubricating the starter.

This side view provides details of the rear brake pedal and the right foot board. Behind the pedal is the clutch link. The lower end of the front safety guard is bolted to the frame at the right of the photo.

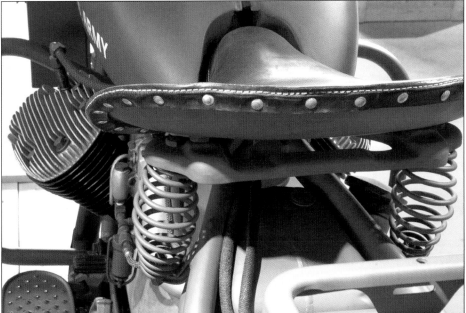

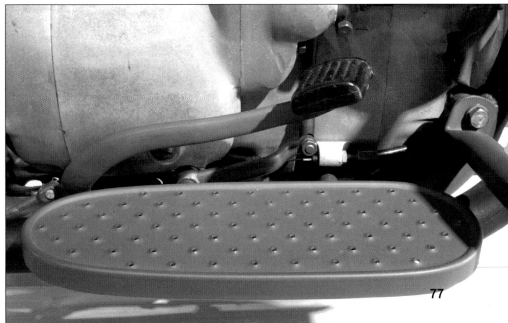

Featured here is a downward view of the blackout and service tail/brake lights and their wiring connectors. Below the fender is the rear guard extension, which bolts to the rear of the frame. Extending below this extension (below the bottom of the fender) is the brace that supports the rear of the left muffler (a similar brace supports the right muffler).

The standard armament of the motorcycle messenger was the Thompson submachine gun. This M1 Thompson submachine gun was adopted for US service in 1942 and replaced the previous and similar looking M1928A1 Thompson. Before WWII's end, the M1 was replaced by the simpler M1A1 Thompson. (Rock Island Arsenal Museum)

With classic looks, noted reliability, and easy access to ammunition (the Thompson fired the same ammunition as the M1911A1 pistol) the "Tommy gun" was a favorite of many GIs, especially motorcycle troops, who did not have to physically carry the relatively heavy weapon. (Rock Island Arsenal Museum)

The filler cap for the oil tank, stamped "OIL," is below the saddle. The maintenance manual for the Model 841 recommended that the oil bath air cleaner (to the right of the oil tank) be removed, cleaned, and refilled with clean motor oil (same grade used in the engine) each time the engine oil was changed.

Data Tables

Harley-Davidson XA: General Data

Model	XA
Weight Net	525 lb.
Wheelbase	59.5 in.
Tire Size	4.00-18
Fuel Capacity	4½ gallons
Electrical	6 Volt negative ground
Transmission Speeds	4 FWD

Harley-Davidson XA: Engine Data

Engine Make/Model	Harley-Davidson
Number of Cylinders	2
Cubic Inch Displacement	45
Horsepower	23 @ 4,500 rpm

Harley-Davidson WLA: General Data

Model	WLA
Weight	513 lb.
Length	88 in.
Width	36.25 in.
Height	59 in.
Wheelbase	50.75 in.
Tire Size	4.00-18
Max. Speed	70 mph
Fuel Capacity	3⅜ gallons
Range	124
Electrical	6 Volt negative ground
Transmission Speeds	3
Turning Radius (feet)	7 right, 7.5 left

Harley Davidson WLA: Engine Data

Engine Make/Model	Harley-Davidson WLA
Number of Cylinders	45 Degree V-2
Cubic Inch Displacement	45
Horsepower	23@4,600 rpm
Torque	28@3,000 rpm
Governed Speed (rpm)	Not Governed

Harley-Davidson U & UA: General Data

Model	U & UA
Weight	850 lb.
Length	95 in.
Width	69 in.
Height	42 in.
Wheelbase	59.5
Tire Size	4.50-18
Max.Speed	55 mph
Electrical	6 Volt negative ground
Transmission Speeds	3

Harley-Davidson U & UA: Engine Data

Engine Make/Model	Harley-Davidson U
Number of Cylinders	45 Degree V-2
Cubic Inch Displacement	74
Horsepower	34 @ 4,000 rpm

Harley-Davidson U

Indian 340-B with Sidecar: General Data

Model	340-B with sidecar
Weight	845 lb. with sidecar
Length	97.5 in.
Width	88.5 in
Height	44 in.
Wheelbase	61.5 in.
Tire Size	4.00-18
Max. Speed	not to exceed 65 mph
Fuel Capacity	3½ gallons
Electrical	6 Volt negative ground
Transmission Speeds	3

Indian 340-B with Sidecar: Engine Data

Engine Make/Model	Indian
Number of Cylinders	42 Degree V-2
Cubic Inch Displacement	73.625
Horsepower	40

Indian 841: General Data

Model	841
Weight	550 lb.
Max. Speed	7o mph
Electrical	6 Volt negative ground
Transmission Speeds	4

Indian 841: Engine Data

Engine Make/Model	Indian
Number of Cylinders	90 degree V-2
Cubic Inch Displacement	45
Horsepower	24 @ 4,000 rpm